Blessings

Words
Inspired,
Imagined
and Revealed

A selection of original works

Manon Joice

BALBOA.
PRESS
A DIVISION OF HAY HOUSE

ISBN: 9781452560441 (sc)
ISBN: 9781452560458 (e)

Library of Congress Control Number: 2012918865

Balboa Press books may be ordered through booksellers or by contacting:

Balboa Press
A Division of Hay House
1663 Liberty Drive
Bloomington, IN 47403
www.balboapress.com
1-(877) 407-4847

Because of the dynamic nature of the Internet, any web addresses or links contained in this book may have changed since publication and may no longer be valid. The views expressed in this work are solely those of the author and do not necessarily reflect the views of the publisher, and the publisher hereby disclaims any responsibility for them.

The author of this book does not dispense medical advice or prescribe the use of any technique as a form of treatment for physical, emotional, or medical problems without the advice of a physician, either directly or indirectly. The intent of the author is only to offer information of a general nature to help you in your quest for emotional and spiritual well-being. In the event you use any of the information in this book for yourself, which is your constitutional right, the author and the publisher assume no responsibility for your actions.

Any people depicted in stock imagery provided by Thinkstock are models, and such images are being used for illustrative purposes only.
Certain stock imagery © Thinkstock.

Printed in the United States of America

Balboa Press rev. date: 10/05/2012

To my beloved mother,
ils fait longtemps que je t'aime, jamais je ne t'oublierai

TABLE OF CONTENTS

Book 1

Book Two

Book 1

This first effort at publishing my own written works represents a selection of personal favorites from poems, prose, prayers, devotionals and news articles I have written over many years. For those who have helped instill in me a love for the written and spoken word, and offered their encouragement I am most grateful. Through their inspiration by example and a gentle prod they have helped to provide me with the confidence to embark upon this venture.

Manon Joice

GIFT OF SILENCE

I love that God is mute
When I pray to him I know from his stillness
He believes in me and has the faith in my abilities
To find my own way

Because of this I cherish prayer
That tiny space of time when God himself
Is just listening and hearing
What I need to say

With no judgement, no suggestion
Just a quiet knowing
A bond of trust between us
Tells me I am okay

When Angels Sing Your Name

When angels sing your name my son
You will know it is time to go
Our first father will claim your spirit
And flesh will be no more

When the angels sing your name
Reach for the brightest star
For in her bosom you will find
Serenity from afar

She will hold and caress you
As gently as did I
But unlike me remove your pain
To let your spirit fly

And when the angels sing your name
Embrace their peacefulness
Let go my hand and you will have
A life beyond all this

I heard the angels sing your name
I know you did too
You heeded all I said my son
Now I will mourn for you

I will long for you each lonely day
Until my time arrives
For when you left my little one
My soul most surely died

And when the angels sing my name
I will reach the brightest star
He will be you my first born son
To take me where you are

On Love

The act of love is
Leading one gently back to themselves

THE CHAIR

The chair where one last sat
Is now empty
For she did not come back
The chair turns grey
Its colour fades
It has collected dust
For it has not been touched
No one shall ever sit there again
After the owner has fled
Her glasses remain
Near a table end
They too grow old with dust
Representing years of being untouched
Listen closely what do you hear?
Her voice so clear
The answer is impossible
For she is dead my dear
Look!
There's her figure I see
Or do I?

A memory flies by
So hard to believe
So lifelike indeed
For I went to touch her
Only to have my hand slip
Feeling the chair where she did sit
My hand swished through the air
Now covered in dust
As it should
When there is no one to touch
Her eyes alive I swore
But their darkness grew cold
Her hair also dark
And shining as always
Will the picture remain?
No the picture fades
I weep
Oh to be close to her
As I use to be
My eyes are watery
They represent the pain
Of her memory

THANK YOU

The two of you together
His tiny hand in yours

The hugs you share
Your love is there

All this make me
Love you more

And I could never dream
A better father for my son

I give thanks everyday
For me you are the one

THE GIFT

If I gave you a pen, only one
With no promise
As to the amount of ink,

Would you write a love letter
Begin a masterpiece
Or scribble a doodle?

Would you write a new sonnet
Draw a cartoon
And share it?

Or instead, would you save it
Hide it and hold it close
Fearing to waste the precious ink?

Now what would you do
If I gave you
A life?

Reflection

When God shows me the light
He is revealing my inner self to me
I in turn am ready and willing to face him
Yes, worthy of him and all his glory
All his wonder, delight and times amusement
I am willing to be one with him again and in turn
I am willing to be me
That authentic self
Stripped of all the layers of life
Guilt, shame
Unworthiness and ego
I am as him with him united in one pure love
Love being the only matter that exists
As such all the matter I access
By will, pure will and desire and belief
It is divinity to see outside ourselves
That pure love which is within

ELISE

Standing stoic at the edge of the cliff,
The cold wind and light rain
Struck her face like tiny shards of glass

Not wavering, she defiantly chose
To withstand nature's elements
And endure her punishment

Her long black gown
Weighed heavy in the storm
Now wet, she turned and walked towards her accusers

The crowd stood motionless as she neared
Once past,
She reached the wooden crate

With long blanched fingers
She stroked the wet case
That held her husband's cold remains

Fulfillment

The pursuit of the material world is a false shield to the
reality of the universe. It is a false joy and always temporary.
There is no happier heart or more joyful soul than the one
who can stand alone. Naked of all possessions and titles
and can stand alone to say, "I am filled with the grace of
God". I have all that I need and desire because I am filled
with love and that love radiates through me. It is whole and
wholesome and never ending. It is this love that validates me,
my purpose and my existence and it is more than enough.

Until

Until the sky has lost all its blue
And no more dreams can come true
I'll be loving you

Until the sun no longer is warming
And the earth itself now is mourning
I'll be loving you

Until the daylight turns only to night
And the stars no longer are bright
I'll be loving you

Until the river no longer is raging
And the world has stopped aging
I'll be loving you

Until the moon has lost all its mystery
And the earth itself now is thirsty
I'll be loving you

Until the earth becomes just dust
And the heavens no longer engage us
I'll be loving you

Until the mighty mountains crumble
And man no longer is humble
I'll be loving you

Faith

I wonder what God must be doing right now
Sometimes I think he must laugh at us
For we look so amusing in our confusion
Other times he must be very sad
For all our pain and suffering

I know he must rejoice
In all our discoveries and joy
I know he loves me and my family
And with that no eternal harm will come

Thank you God for this day
Help me make the most of it
Amen

FORGIVENESS

It is only when we forgive the past
That we have a future

LOVE

Love is personal
As individual as you and I
And its' intentions boundless

I Miss you Still

I miss you still
Though thirteen years
Since last I kissed your cheek

I'm no longer young
Or so it seems
As life has aged in me

I grew up strong,
Told I'm like you
That was all I wanted to be

For in doing so
Dear mom
I held your memory

But through it all
Not much has changed
For I grew up to be

A lonely girl
Still reaching back
For her mother to cradle me

Take Him Not

Take him not my love from me

Take instead the breath I breathe
Not because I am strong
But because I am weak

Take him not my love from me

There is no place I long to be
Without my first love my last love
The very life I breathe

Take him not my love from me

Without his face I wish not see
Without his touch I do not feel
This world around I will not need

Take him not my love from me

JUDGMENT

Don't judge where one has been
Instead see where he is going

Desires

Our wants are merely distractions to our needs

THE DAY WILL COME

When war will be no more
When hunger will cease
And our souls rejoice
As never before

All men will sing in harmony
Conducted by one father
And no more will there be
Suffering for each other

Oh Dear God Why Am I Here?

At time I believe my naivety leads to your amusement
This cannot be why I am here
Help me to hear you, to feel you
Even to be you
Help me to see what I am meant to be
To do what I am meant to do
Help me to fulfill my life mission
I need clarity, I need objectivity and simplicity
Only you can provide all three
But I need the path to be seen before me
Adjust my eyes and clear my vision
De-cloud my mind so that I may be one with you,
One with me and one with all around me

How to Love

Love me like that
Wholly
Verbally and spiritually
And I will remember you

Show me your world
And open my eyes
To all that matters to you

Let it be that in that moment
You will remember me too

Fears Behind

I see you in the dark
But light still surrounds us

I feel the touch
And the warmth of your smile

I want you near
With nothing between us

We will leave our fears behind

I know the fear
Of love and compassion

I've run away
From the look in your eyes

You will never know
How much I adore you

Help me leave my fears behind

Dear God

I hope we all can see our ability to love each other
and ourselves
That is all in truth we need to do to love you
I understand you ask this of us not out of
selfishness for worship
But for our own entire well being
As a universe as a people and as a community
Help us to see what we need to do
In order to attain this utopia
And give us the courage and yes the means to see it through
Help us make our vision and your vision come to fruition
With love and appreciation for this day and everyday
Amen

Soul Journey

The more I fail in society the truer I am to my soul

The Earth

The earth in all its glory
Is made more beautiful
Through you and I

If we see its magnificence
We see our majestic selves
The ones who decide where this beauty lies

So believe me when I say
Whether glorious or bleak
We made it so by the ambitions that we seek

I LOVE YOU

I love you
A phrase more often
Said than any other

But when you say it to me
It is as innocent and true
As though spoken for the first time

I believe you
And
Your words

CONCEPTION

When I see you marvel at him
With adoration and love

I cannot help but remember
The first time we touched
The first time you kissed me
Held me close and we loved

Only the beginning of what was to come
And now he is here our firstborn son
And in him we planted the memory
Of this, our everlasting love

SPEAK

Say you love me
Not with your gaze
Or kind gestures
But use your words
Tell me now

ABUNDANCE

For all those who know
The precious gift of a kiss
You are the wealthy

For all those who experience
A hug from your child
You are the fortunate

For all of those immersed
In love from another
You are the boundless

All of you are victorious
You have experienced life's greatest achievement
Truth, Innocence, Joy and Bliss

And all this can be found only in the presence of each other

Serving God

You are obedient to God and serve him best
When you live your hearts desires

Death and Dying

Death and dying are very frightful to many in our society. We do not know what all the universe entails as the end of life and of breathe leads to the mysteries of the afterlife and hence life itself. It is ridiculous to assume that our only reason for existence is to gather the necessities for our survival. These include food, clothing and shelter. They also include protection. This protection is a new concept. It is the protection from harm and death we seek and we aimlessly go about trying to attain this armour for ourselves. We attempt to deny aging and slow it down or hide it through surgery and other masks of illusion. Imagine the time and energy spared in our lives if we only accepted the inevitable and savoured the moment of life. For example, smiling at the sunset, really tasting water, really holding and trusting another. Instead we use our precious time on earth while still healthy stitched up, mutilated and harmed to prevent the harm and mutilation we feared to begin with. Are we so lost that all our energies are to preserve instead of grasp life which is already present? It is a futile attempt to defy the laws of nature. It is worse our rejecting the possibility that something more wondrous awaits us after we expire here on earth. It is so limiting and naïve to think God in all his glory created you and the universe only to extinguish it. We do not extinguish as a flame but are recaptured and realigned and transformed to something greater and more wondrous. Energy does not disappear hence our being our souls in their great form of pure energy cannot entirely expire.

We instead transcend and if we believe this were so we would have no fear or difficulty in holding on to what we know here on earth. In turn we would savour the moment instead of trying to manipulate it. Trust in God and trust in yourself when you believe you are here forever.

The question than is, what are we here for? The answer maybe for whatever you want. You were given senses desire and creativity. This is a playground for exploration and experiences. Love, hate, fear, rage, compassion and joy; all these and many more emotions exist for you on this plane. You were created to experience them all not just one or two. You are personality and persona, a reflection of your experiences, your desires and most importantly your dreams. God imagines more for you than you can see. He is not limited by time, space or fear. The world is only filled with endless possibility and you were given the power to create your own existence. This existence lies in the here and now

LOSS THROUGH SUICIDE

Suicide has shattering meaning to those who are here on earth. It is a common belief that suicide leads to never-ending suffering for those who are gone and for those left here to grieve. The act of suicide is the symbol of failure. The failure to see, the failure to trust and the failure to hope. It is also the failure to lave and trust in the love that surrounds us all.

As such, it is easy for those who have lost a loved one to suicide to feel abandoned, rejected and guilty. These emotions also include anger. We need to release our anger and thus our loved one. It is this anger which taints us into accepting the possibility that our loved one exists in a place we call hell. This hell we create is dark and frightening and painful. It is the accumulation of our worst fears and suffering and in turn, our grief.

What if for just a moment instead, we imagined our loved one, their soul in a place that is free from harm, pain and suffering. It is light, it is accepting, it is nurturing, wholesome and healing . Is this not, after all, what we wanted to create for them on earth but feel we failed to do so?

Why then continue to bind ourselves? Instead we can choose to finally provide that safe haven, that heaven which in turn releases us from guilt, pain and shame. It is trust that will allow you to create this place for those you have lost.

Trust you can put them there and they will indeed be there. Use your love, your energy and your desire to create this and wonderful existence and it will be so.

LIVING A NEW NORMAL

A swift reminder of our loss or suffering is the new and altered state of our lives. It is no wonder many who have endured the loss of a loved one or who have survived terrible ordeals have a tendency to take in their altered life, one step at a time. Often finding themselves moving slowly, in a world that is quickly changing shape.

It is common to find yourself nibbling at food, taking longer to complete mundane tasks and wondering where the days have gone. Not only do we experience great fatigue but emotionally, we need time to adjust to our new normal. We may be eating dinner alone for the first time, we may be doing laundry for one less child or we may be learning to walk with a new prosthetic. All these dramatic changes to our daily lives act as a weight we carry. They remind us we are not the same. It is no wonder we move slower. We are slower to act and to react. We are off balance in our new world and thus move forward only with deliberate and measured paces.

As time passes, however you come to find through repetition, that those mundane tasks of everyday life now altered forever become the new normal. When this takes place you will expand, absorbing other experiences life has to offer. In your time, this transition will lead you to a new existence. Growing, in directions you may never imagine. Is it a better way of life than that of the one you had before, no. Is it a better way of life than that you had envisioned for your future, again no. It is however your new normal and in this new life lies your testimony to your experience with loss and pain.

The world is changing and transforming and so are you. It can be a very painful transition to this new normal way of life. It is in the living of this new normal you will find joy, peace, and purpose once again. This is not to suggest you let go of who you were or who you lost, but instead carry with you the memories, the spirit and the hope of your loved one for strength as you forge through this new beginning.

HAPPINESS

Through conversations with many and again recently, there comes the notion of forgiveness. Forgiveness to me is the real secret to happiness. The question, however, remains- what is true forgiveness and how does one forgive truly.

For myself, true forgiveness occurs when one is no longer burdened by the actions of another. We have all been wronged by another and there is no action that one person can commit that another can't forgive. One important key is to remember the sense of justice we, as persons, feel must be done. It is this need that limits us. We want redemption, and compensation from the other, but this rarely occurs, at least directly, to those who have been harmed. Expect nothing and you won't be disappointed, forgive them anyway. It is their weakness and not yours. Remember always: this world may not be fair, but a greater spirit is and should you look very closely, you will recognize that justice takes many forms.

It is said one loves to the extent one forgives. This is very true. One cannot expect to be in the right if they hold resentment towards another and it is that resentment, that burden one bears when they do not forgive. There will come a point however, when you truly forgive another person, when the sadness you feel is for them and not for yourself and that is forgiveness. When you can view a situation as a test to ensure you will not change who you are, you can proclaim, I will remain true to myself, my spirit, and my God not because of all that has happened but despite it. I will remain loving, caring, and forgiving and for that I will retain eternal *happiness.*

GRIEF AND HOPE

With hope we will move forward not because of our loss
but despite it. This hope for ourselves, our loved ones and
our neighbors lies only in our future. It is our hope in
tomorrow that allows us to cope with our loss of today.

Book Two

This second effort at publishing my own written works represents a selection of personal favorites from poems, prose, prayers and devotionals I have written since my last collection. For those who have supported me in my last effort and continue to encourage me in my writing, I remain eternally grateful. It is through your strength and encouragement that I remain inspired and fearless in my craft. With your love and God's love my dreams have been manifested. Know I am thankful for all my gifts, most especially, the gifts of friendship, faith and family.

Manon Joice

RED ROBIN

The robin
With red breast
Appears to me
When at my best
A sign from heaven
A promise from above
Reminding me always
I am still loved

OF EMILY DICKENSON

Her talent bleeds
On every page
Through every word
She has written

MIDNIGHT MAUVE

Midnight mauve
Is the colour I see
When I meditate

I am closer to God
When surrounded
By this hue

I hear him whisper to me
I remember when I held his hand
Before being born

I am safe and content
I am who I am
Meant to be

Today, I close my eyes
To remember
This delicate tone

To remember being safe and
Trusting in my future
While rejoicing in my past

All is forgiven
All is for purpose
All is in Midnight Mauve

Because of You

When I see you
I believe
You alone are responsible
For placing each star,
The moon
And the
Northern Lights
In perfect arrangement
Just for my eyes to see
I am in awe
Of you
And all that is
Around me

CHILD OF GOD

If you ridicule yourself,
Judge yourself
And are unkind to yourself
Ask yourself,
Who are you
To treat a child of God
So harshly

MIRACLES

You too can cause
Miracles
Each dream you
Manifest
Each movement that you
Make
All conspire to
Create
The life you so
Desire
God made you in his
Image
And gave you his
Talents
To demonstrate you are
Capable
Of forming a world perfect
Just for you

IMAGINATION

Imagination
The gift of creation
Makes us each unique
It is in this moment
Our dreams spill over
To what we can achieve

DREAMS

The whispers from angels
A gentle prod
Dreams they remind us
We are of God

Manifest

Create and manifest
Know it is true
All this is possible
Because of you

No Remorse

Should you leave tomorrow
Through death, divorce
Or you stray

Know I will not regret you
Or the times we shared
Till this day

Know I will forgive your absence
And never begrudge
Your leaving

Be certain instead I will remember
The joys
We experienced

Know each moment with you was a gift
An unexpected surprise morn after morn
When we awoke still together

And because this is so
I now know that dreams can come true
Even if you should go away

Nonetheless my greatest dream yet
Would be to have
You stay

JOY

Joy to move stretch and breathe
Joy to know you believe

Joy to sing dance and pray
Joy to know a glorious day

Joy to give thanks praise and love
Joy illumes each of us

Three Crosses

Three crosses that stand
As tall as three towers

Reminding us all
Of the one final hour

When all is forgiven
Of the strong and the meek

For sins committed
Against the one that we seek

Do not forget
Of the great sacrifice

That afforded to us
Long lasting life

Paid by one
A very high price

ANGELS

I feel the flutter of soft wings
I know they surround me

I hear them whisper in my dreams
I know they surround me

I imagine great things
I know they surround me

I see miracles abound
I know they surround me

They inspire me
I know they surround me

Because I believe
They surround me

HIGHER

Dreams like prayers are from our higher selves but to put these in motion you need to make them happen here on earth on this plane. Only you mortals understand the net workings of your existence the complex rationales you impose upon your own possibilities which are limitless. You are boundless your intentions are your experiences and as such you must intend for the highest good for yourselves and those around you if you are to succeed in achieving peace, tranquility, success, delight and joy. Bliss is possible for you for anyone who believes in the power of their dream, of their prayer, of their power here on earth. Together with the help of your guides, your angels, your creator all is possible you need only to take the first step towards self actualization and you in your most glorified form will be realized.

Remember you can become your higher self imagine your most beautiful blue, graceful face attached to a most large and   beautiful body winged and ready for a anything because you are impermeable.

CHANGE

Change can lead us to be nervous and uncertain. We are wandering upon new grounds in this day, in this time. Readings we memorized are now becoming anew as we see the true meaning in them. Their intention to inspire, delight and make aware the circumstances that surround us. With light, the light of love and understanding and yes openness we see a new beginning for ourselves, our children and our grandchildren. We also find new hope for those loved ones who have already moved forward. This knowledge emerges as new but believe and trust it was always before you, meant to be the constant in our lives that gives you the courage and the faith to move forward in your divine existence. Know as you move forward one toe at a time that the water is warm. You will eventually become emerged in this warmth and you too will glow as you realize the warmth comes and radiates from you. You are not alone as you are all one with the greatest power of God. Trust and believe that the one next to you is before you with thought, purpose and reason. In all there is an answer to someone's prayer. Trust and believe these prayers are coming through now faster than before because you are ready to accept the truth. The truth you know is that God resides in you. As such radiates through you. You have nothing to fear. The sea of knowledge is warm it is the lack of understanding that is cold.

GIFT OF WATER

Water buoyant
Carries me

Water balmy
Warms me

Water cool
Nourishes me

Water fresh
Cleanses me

Water waving
Soothes me

Water pouring
Blesses me

Love Divine

Of all celestial gifts
Love is the greatest
And none greater
Than yours and mine
A love divine

GRATITUDE

Appreciate your blessings
For you have many

The air you breathe
The water you drink
The sun you see
All just a beginning

Give thanks for all your wisdom
Through all your joys and grief
It is in these experiences
You become who you are meant to be

RESPONSIBILITY

There is a great paradox
When you realize you are
A precious child of God
Capable of wonderment, desire, and love

You know your gift is to create
A world that can delight you
And now you are accountable
To ensure that it be true

Motherhood

No lovelier gift than a true mother
Unwavering sacrifice for a child

With unlimited love
An unconditional devotion

For a soul
Dearer than any other

MARRIAGE

Be grateful for your mate
Bask in their presence too

Appreciate their gift
As they share their essence with you

Know marriage is like water
Waves are high and low

It is in perseverance
We enjoy the tender flow

Give to your marriage these two gifts
Gratitude and forgiveness

And you will have a union
Of which there is no resistance

Of Children

For each and every child
Know you are a gift

An answer from God
Of a parent's greatest wish

There is no task you cannot do
For there is always much greater in you

No dream you cannot receive
For this is the reason you breathe

The fact you are here
Reminds us all dear

You are evidence
Our miraculous dreams do come true

Maturity

You know when to speak or be silent
You learned to listen not just to hear
You resolve not to judge or begrudge
You mastered forgiveness for each of us
You give without expectation
And are also willing to receive
You recognize you are from heaven
And God resides in thee

Paradox

I am in awe of all around me
I humbled by the mountains
Enchanted by the seas

I am in wonder of blue oceans
And stars that light the night
Our sun forever warming
And a moon that hangs so high

Of animals there are plenty
The mighty and the small
The foliage
And fresh produce

And God he made them all

And in this I ponder too
I am most times a tiny little spec
Insignificant and slight
And yet for me all this was made
What a magnificent delight

COURAGE

Courage is moving forward in faith

VESSEL

Your body is the vessel which takes you to where your dreams lie
Treat this vessel well

TRUE FAITH

True faith is to believe in God as much as God believes in you

CPSIA information can be obtained at www.ICGtesting.com
Printed in the USA
LVOW102140161112

307553LV00002B/5/P

9 781452 560441